The Triplet Book for Cello

Part Two:

First Position,

Chromatic Fingering

by Cassia Harvey

CHP259

©2014 by C. Harvey Publications® All Rights Reserved.

www.charveypublications.com - print books & free sheet music blog
www.learnstrings.com - downloadable books & chamber music

2

Trip to Barking Mill

Thompson, arr. Harvey

3

String Crossing

4

Le Courante Limpide

Burgmuller, arr. Harvey

5

Left-Hand Warm-Up

The Triplet Warm-Up Book, Part Two

6

Bonny in the Dumps

Trad., arr. Harvey

©2014 C. Harvey Publications All Rights Reserved.

7

String Crossing

8

Dumphries House Trad., arr. Harvey

9

Left-Hand Warm-Up

©2014 C. Harvey Publications All Rights Reserved.

10

Shandon Bells
Trad., arr. Harvey

11

String Crossing

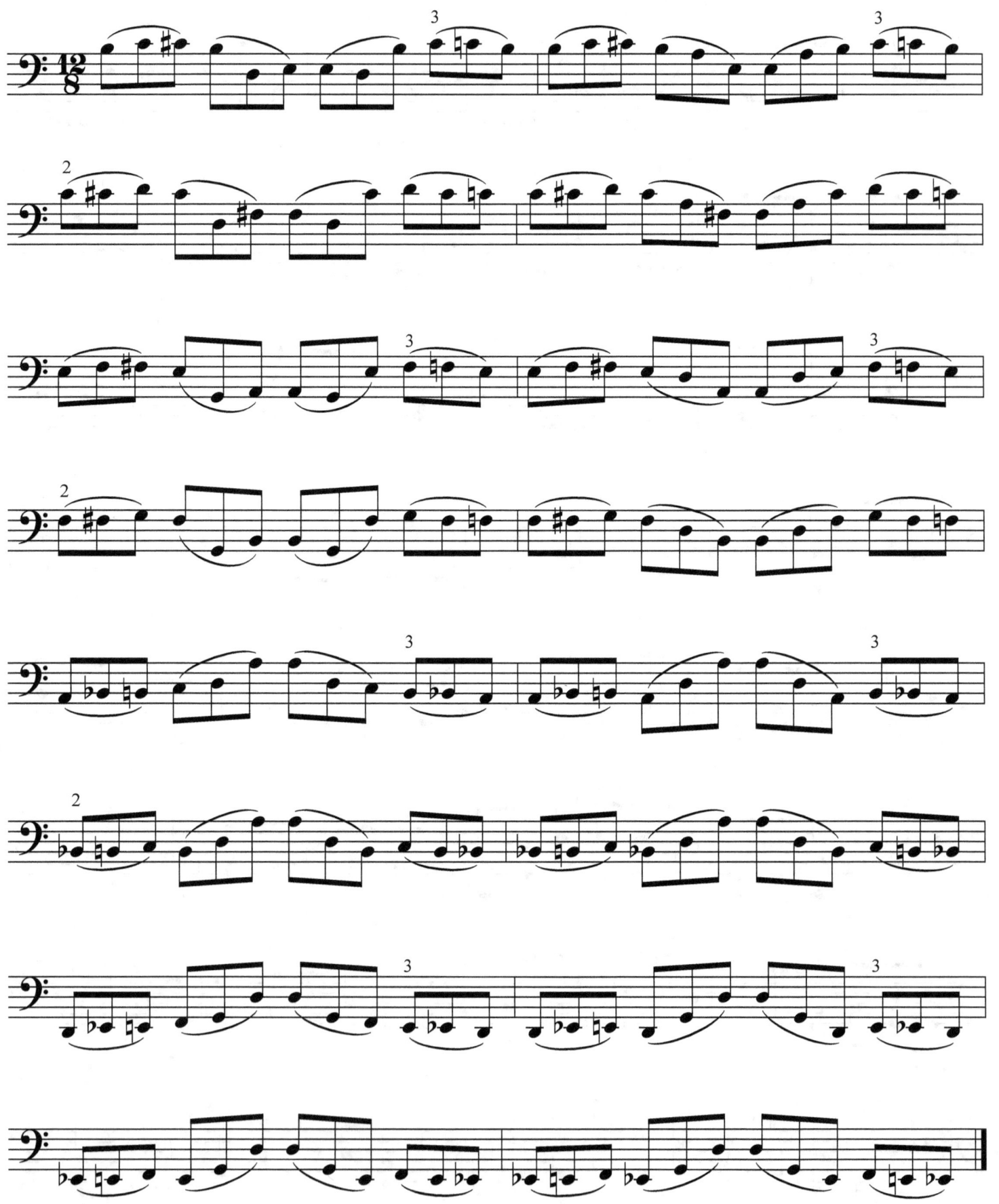

The Triplet Warm-Up Book, Part Two

12

Humors of Glendart

Trad., arr. Harvey

13

Left-Hand Warm-Up

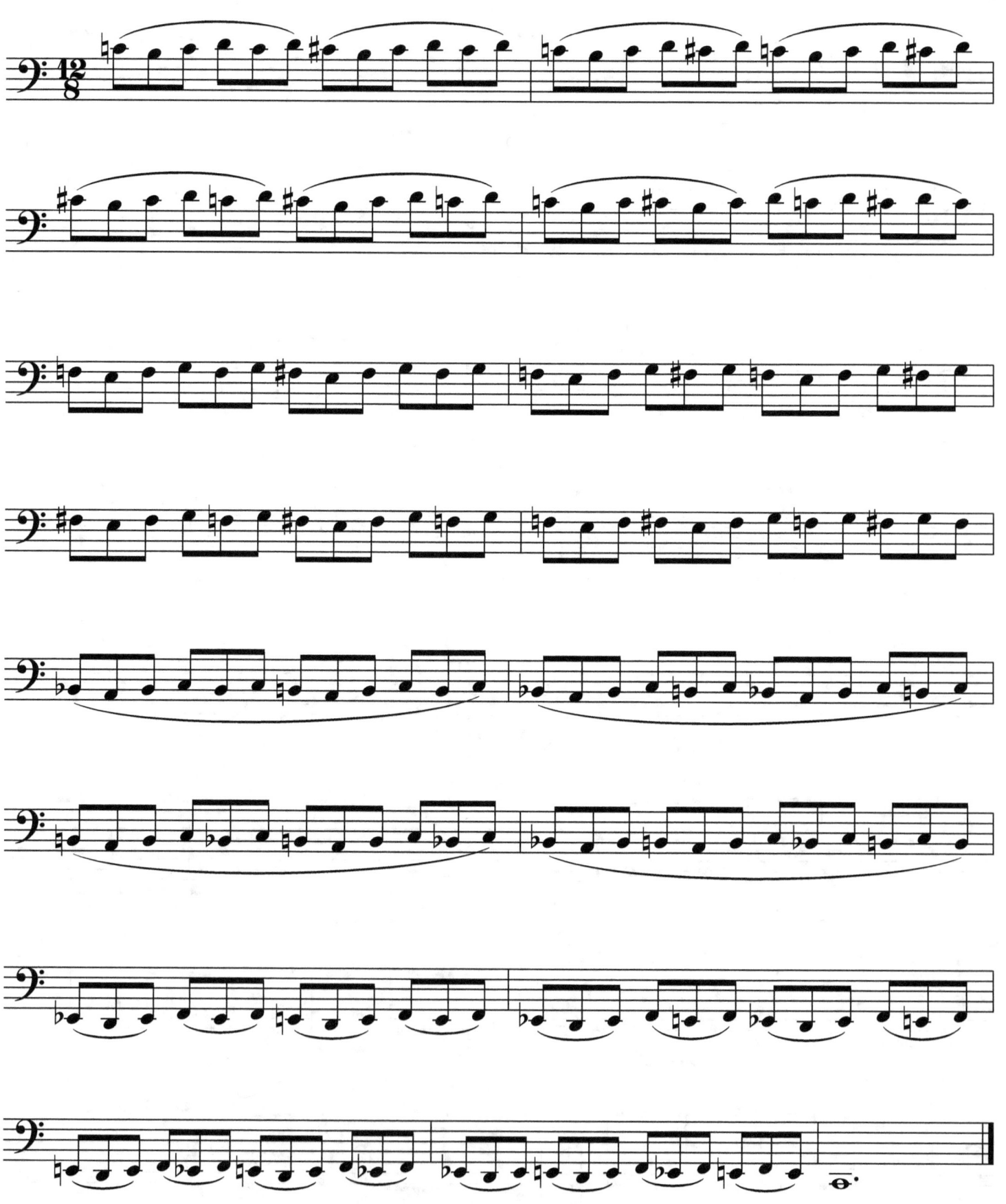

15

String Crossing

The Triplet Warm-Up Book, Part Two

©2014 C. Harvey Publications All Rights Reserved.

16

Galway Tom — Trad., arr. Harvey

17

Left-Hand Warm-Up

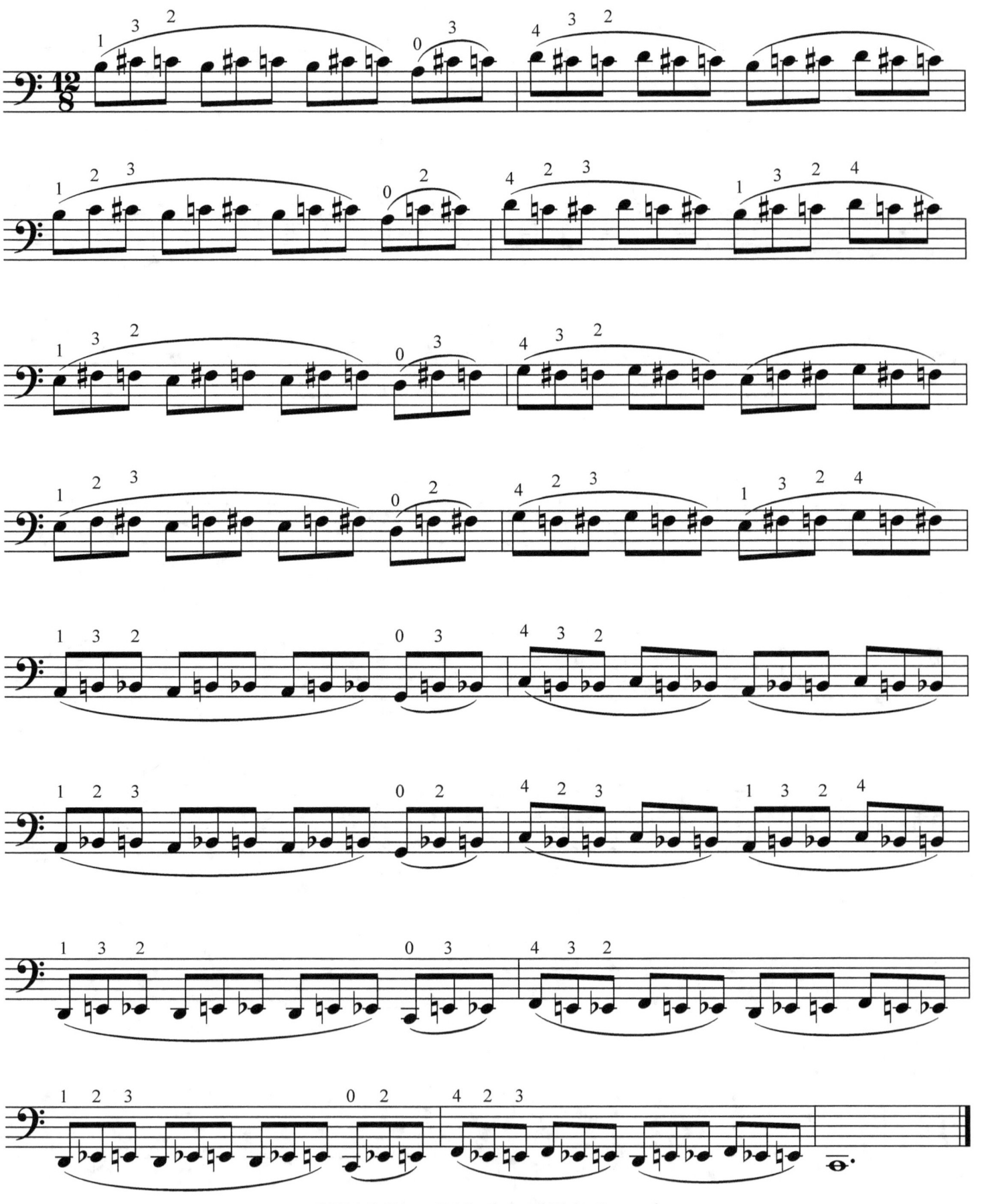

18

Blithe Have I Been Harding, arr. Harvey

19

String Crossing

The Triplet Warm-Up Book, Part Two

20

O'Sullivan's March

Trad., arr. Harvey

©2014 C. Harvey Publications All Rights Reserved.

21

Left-Hand Warm-Up

22

The Humors of Cappa

Trad., arr. Harvey

23

String Crossing

The Triplet Warm-Up Book, Part Two

24

The Book of Rights

Trad., arr. Harvey

©2014 C. Harvey Publications All Rights Reserved.

26

John White's Mother

Trad., arr. Harvey

27

String Crossing

28

The Devil Among the Mealmongers

Trad., arr. Harvey

29

Left-Hand Warm-Up

The Triplet Warm-Up Book, Part Two   31

30

Variations on "For He's a Jolly Good Fellow"   Trad., arr. Harvey

©2014 C. Harvey Publications All Rights Reserved.

31

String Crossing

32

Farewell — Trad., arr. Harvey

33

Left-Hand Warm-Up

The Triplet Warm-Up Book, Part Two

34

The Flora Day Welcome

Bain, arr. Harvey

35

String Crossing

The Triplet Warm-Up Book, Part Two

36

Paddy O'Rafferty Trad., arr. Harvey

©2014 C. Harvey Publications All Rights Reserved.

37

Left-Hand Warm-Up

The Triplet Warm-Up Book, Part Two

38

Spinning Song

Burgmuller, arr. Harvey

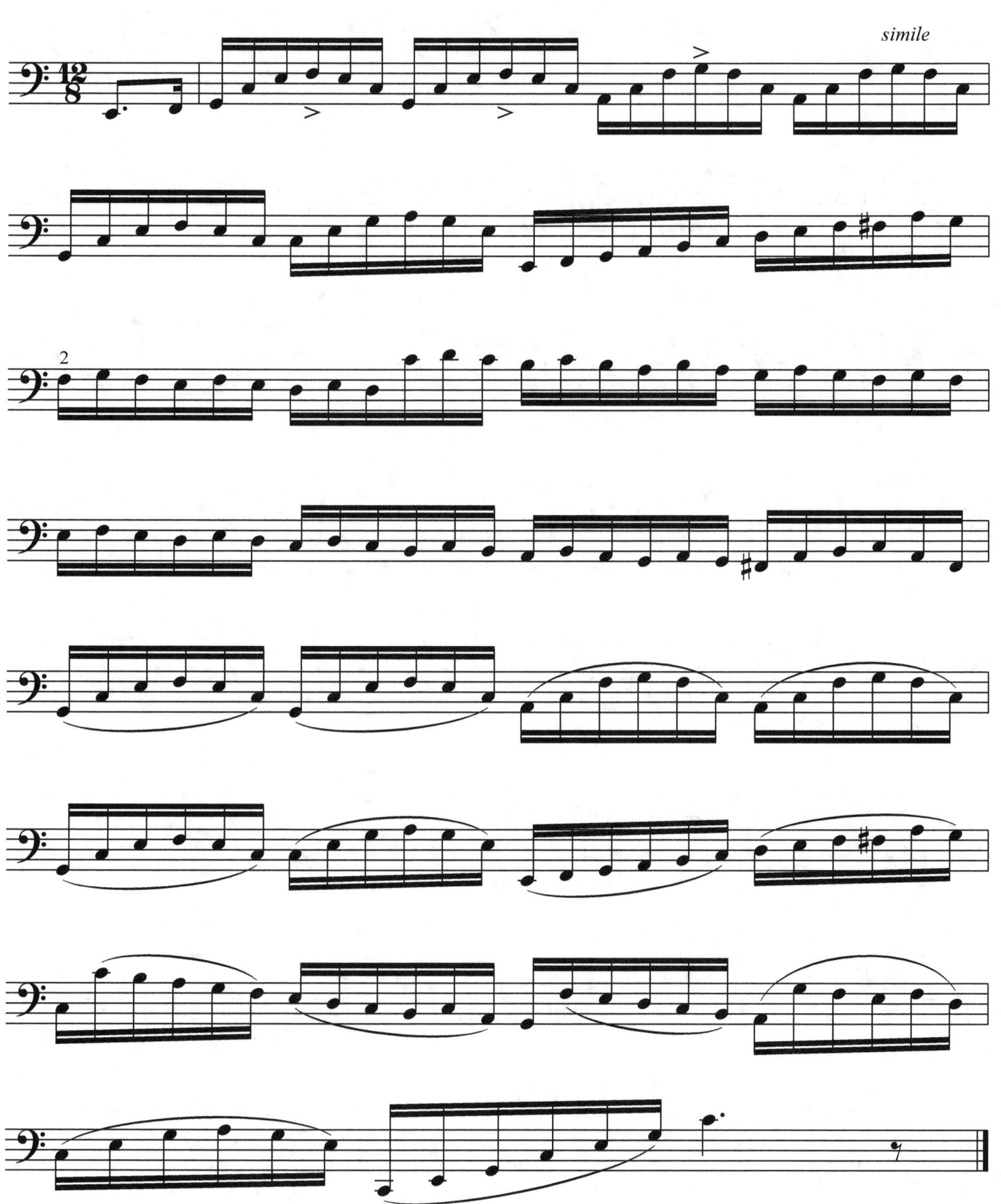

©2014 C. Harvey Publications All Rights Reserved.

39

String Crossing

The Triplet Warm-Up Book, Part Two

41

Left-Hand Warm-Up

©2014 C. Harvey Publications All Rights Reserved.

42

The Tenpenny Piece

Erskine, arr. Harvey

43

String Crossing

44

Le Courant Limpide: Advanced Version

Burgmuller, arr. Harvey

45

Left-Hand Warm-Up

46

String Crossing

47

L'harmonie des Anges

Burgmuller, arr. Harvey

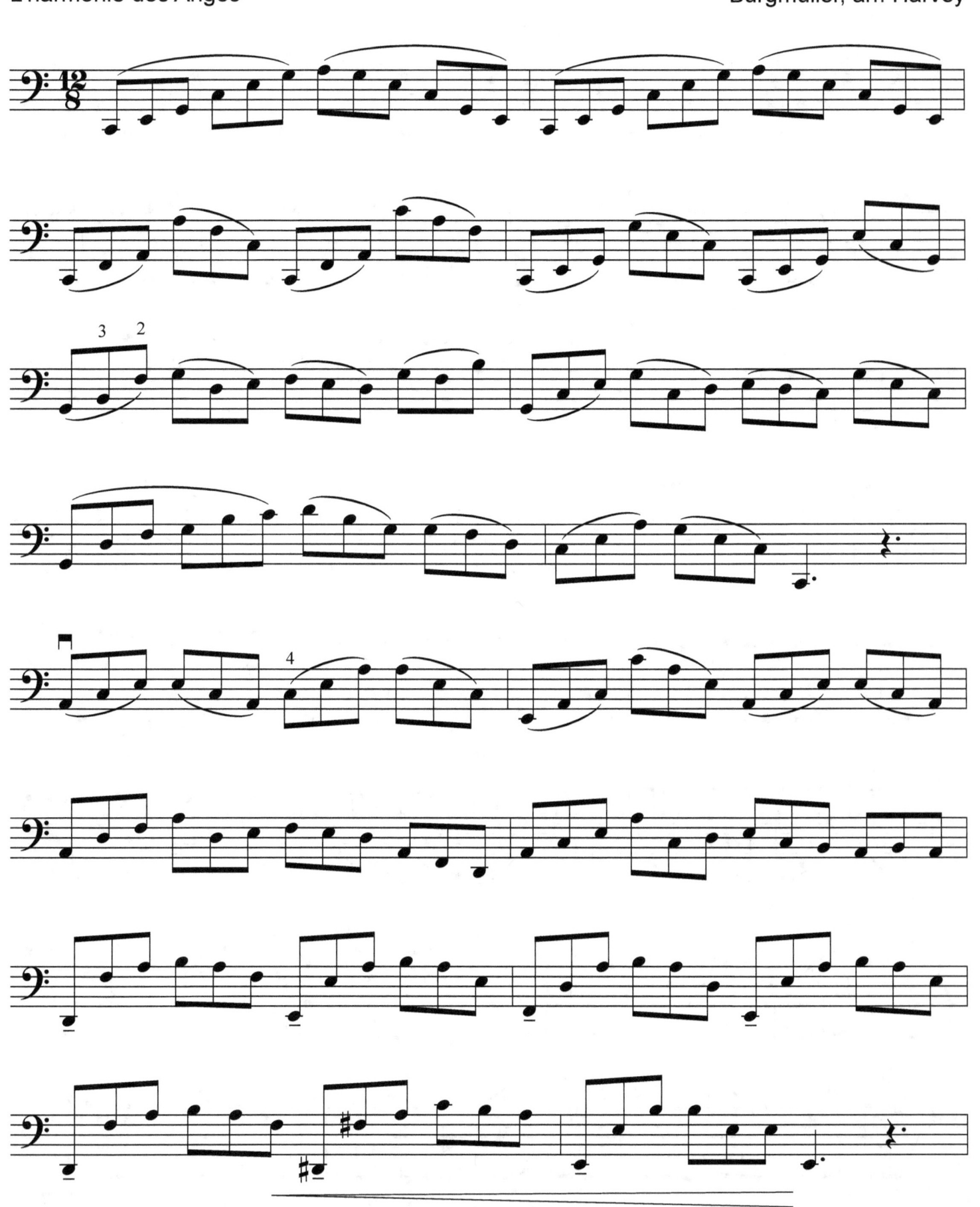

The Triplet Warm-Up Book, Part Two

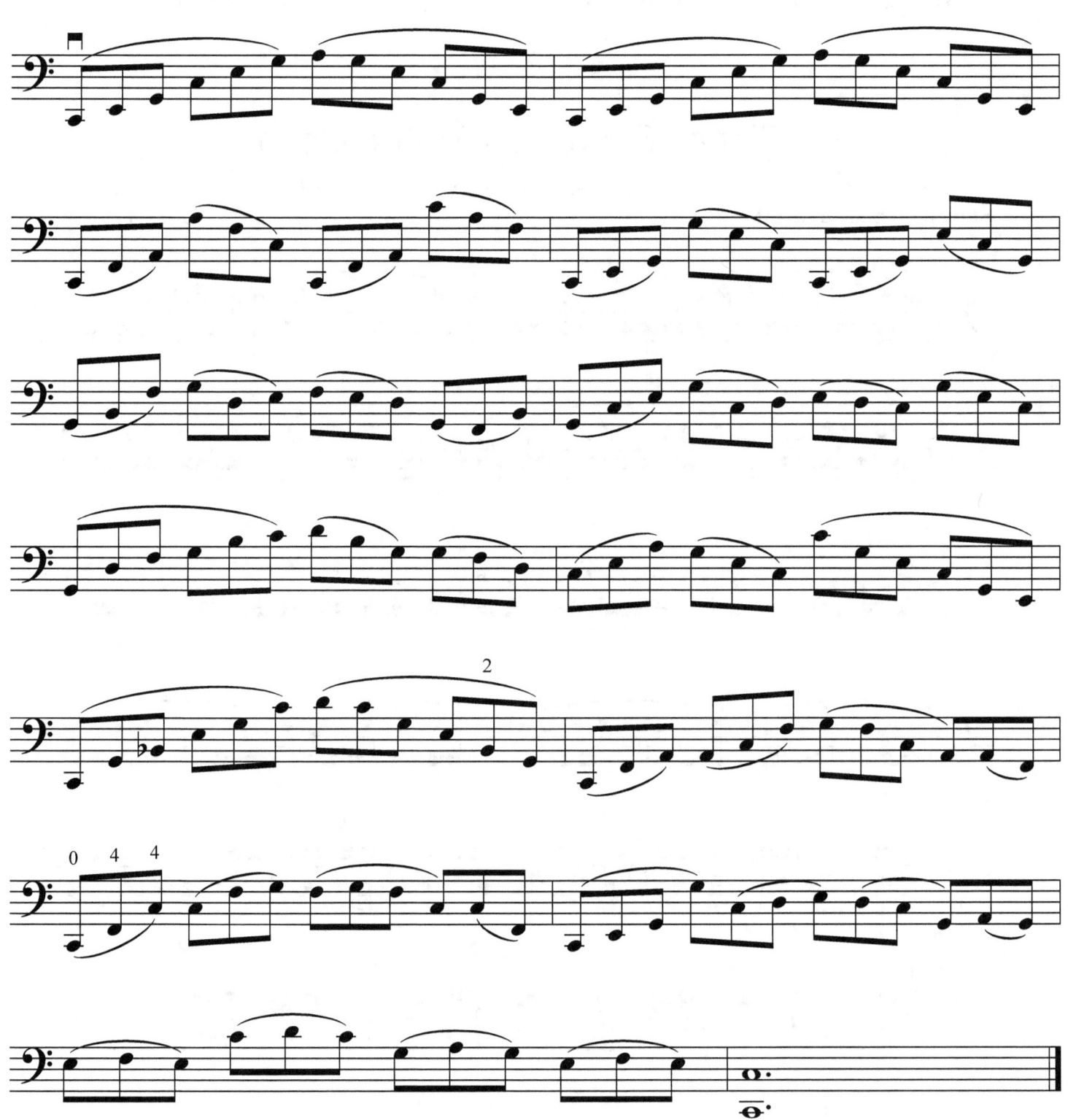

CHP130

Finger Exercises for the Cello
Book Two

Stretching back to a flat

Cassia Harvey

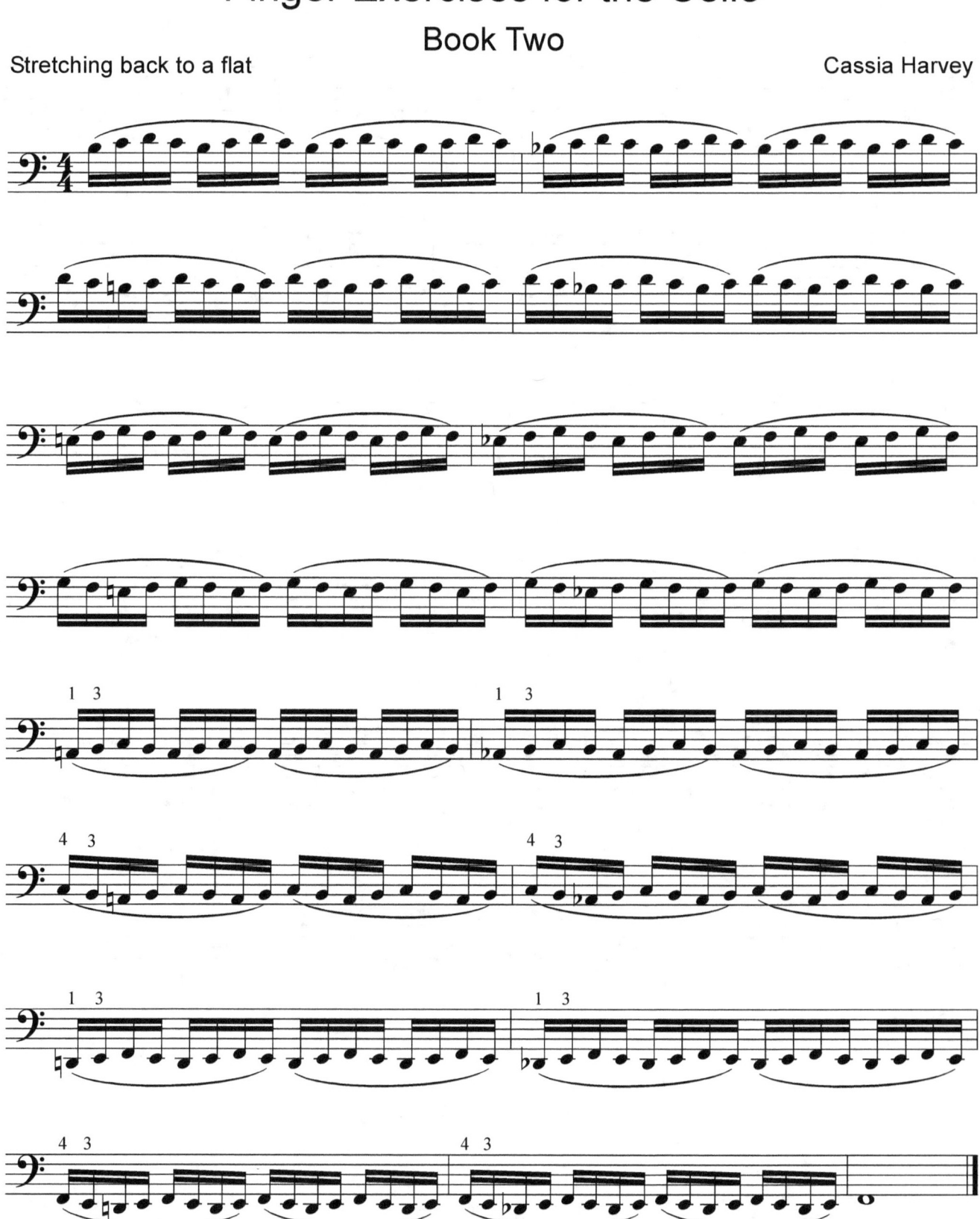

©2005 C. Harvey Publications All Rights Reserved.

www.ingramcontent.com/pod-product-compliance
Lightning Source LLC
Chambersburg PA
CBHW051425070526
44584CB00023B/3584